Genre Expository Text

I0901328

Essential Question
How do people benefit from innovation?

How HORSES Changed the World

by Jane Buxton

Introduction

Who first tamed wild horses? How did wild horses become animals that work for humans? When were they **domesticated**? How has the role of horses changed over time?

Archaeologists, or people who study ancient cultures, think they know some of the answers. They say people first domesticated horses in Kazakhstan and Mongolia about 5,500 years ago.

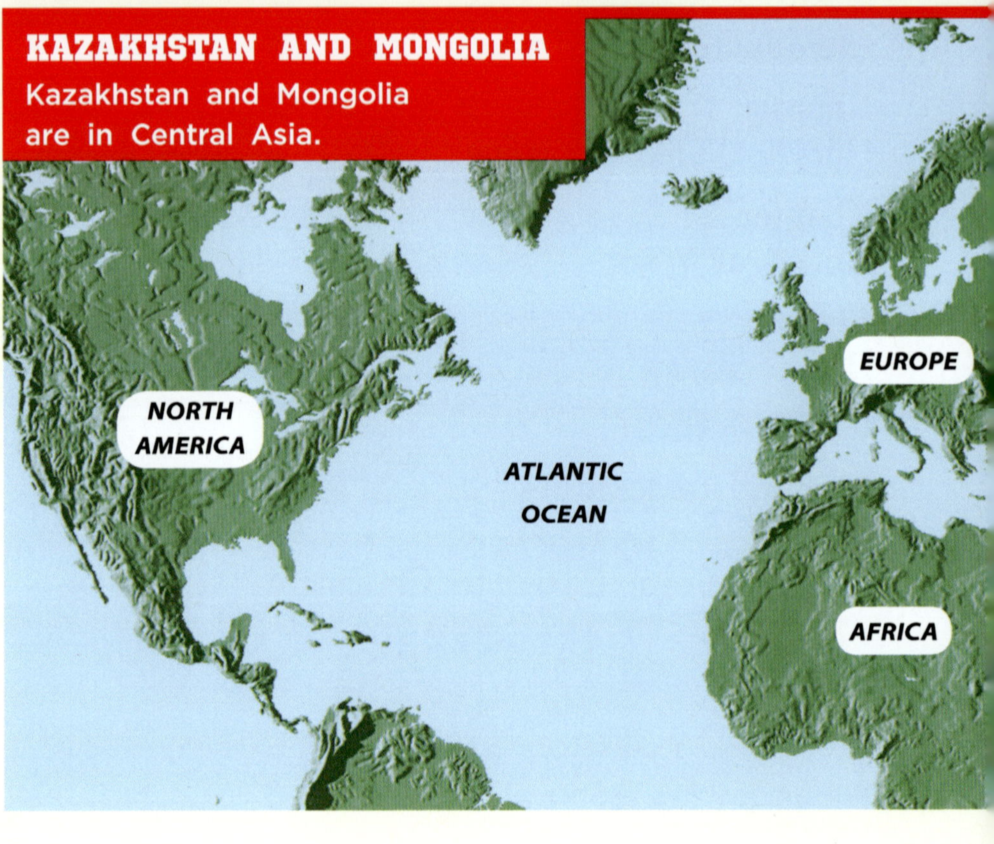

In Kazakhstan, archaeologists have studied ancient pottery. They found fat from horsemeat and from mare's milk on the vessels. This shows that horses were eaten for food and used for their milk.

Archaeologists also found horse teeth that were worn down. This suggests that the animal had held a **bit** in its mouth. People had started riding horses.

Before the **industrial** age, there were no cars or trains. Horses were the best way to carry humans and goods, so people **bred** horses to be fast and strong.

CHAPTER ONE

Horses Widen Horizons

Using horses for transportation led to big changes in people's lives. Groups could travel to find better farmland. When grass was too **sparse** to feed their animals, people could find areas that had more grass.

Fighting in wars changed, too. People on horseback could attack their enemies on the ground from above. Warriors also started using **spoked wheels** on their chariots. Spoked wheels were lighter than solid wheels. This was an important **modification**. It meant that armies could travel farther and faster. This helped them to conquer, or take control of, other lands.

Two-wheeled carts called chariots were used for racing and hunting in ancient Egypt.

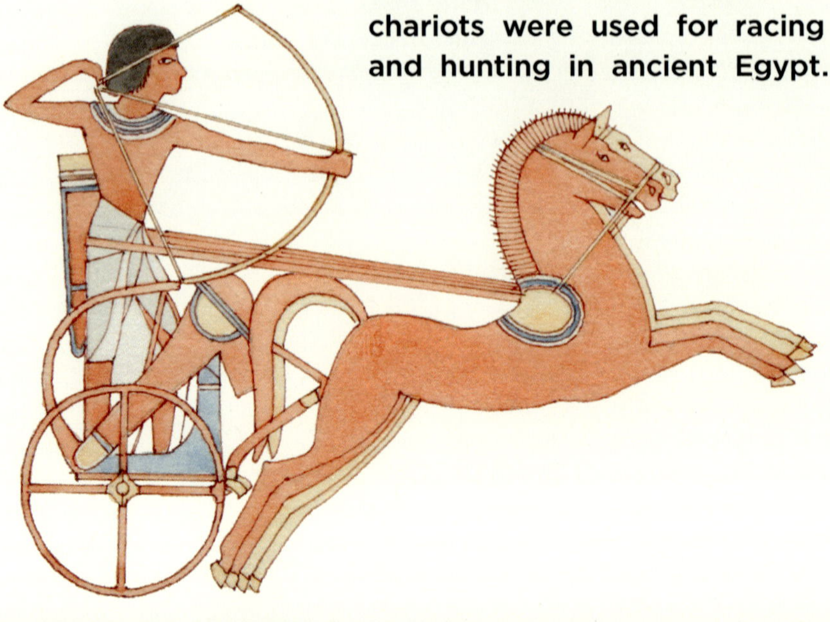

Dorling Kindersley/Getty Images

Alexander the Great, the king of Macedonia, had a big effect on how horses were used in wars. In 334 B.C.E., he led his army out of Greece. The army included 5,000 soldiers on horseback. They traveled thousands of miles and won all their battles. As a result, Alexander's **empire**, the area he ruled, grew substantially bigger.

ALEXANDER & BUCEPHALUS

Alexander the Great had a horse named Bucephalus. Alexander got the horse when someone tried to sell it to his father, the king. Bucephalus was very nervous, so none of the king's horsemen could ride him. Alexander spoke quietly to Bucephalus and calmed him down. Alexander and Bucephalus were close friends from then on.

Life changed for communities that had been invaded. Soldiers settled in conquered lands. They brought new customs. New trading routes were set up, too. As a result, people could get goods from far away.

When the Spanish invaded North America in the 1500s and 1600s, they affected the lives of the Native Americans. The Spanish brought horses with them. Native Americans learned to ride these new animals. They trained and bred them for hunting and warfare. The Spanish horses soon spread across the continent.

Many Spanish horses escaped. Then they lived wild on the open land. The Spanish called these horses *mesteños*, meaning strays, because they lived away from the others. Now they are called mustangs.

The colorful Appaloosas were Native Americans' favorite horses.

Mustangs aren't really wild horses. They are feral horses. "Feral" means they are the **descendants**, or relatives, of domestic horses. But they are now wild.

The only true wild horses live in Mongolia. These horses, called *takhi,* were nearly extinct by 1969. Some were taken to zoos and bred there. Then they were freed from **captivity**, so they are once again wild.

The takhi were first set free on a nature reserve.

STOP AND CHECK

How did horses change how people fought wars?

(b) Nancy G Western Photography, Nancy Greifenhagen/Alamy, (t) Bombaert/iStock/Getty Images

CHAPTER TWO

Horses at Work

For a long time, horses were thought too special to work on farms. But in the 1700s, farmers began to use them. Horses were faster than oxen and donkeys. They also didn't stop to eat while they worked.

In the 1800s, the populations of North America and Europe grew. People needed to grow more crops. They invented bigger and better farm equipment. In the United States, they used large, strong horses to pull the new, heavy farm machinery.

Horses also worked on ranches. People needed to produce more meat, so they set up big cattle ranches in the western United States. Mexican cowboys, called *vaqueros*, worked on the ranches.

The vaqueros used horses to herd the cattle to fresh pastures and distant markets. They also used horses to stop cattle from straying.

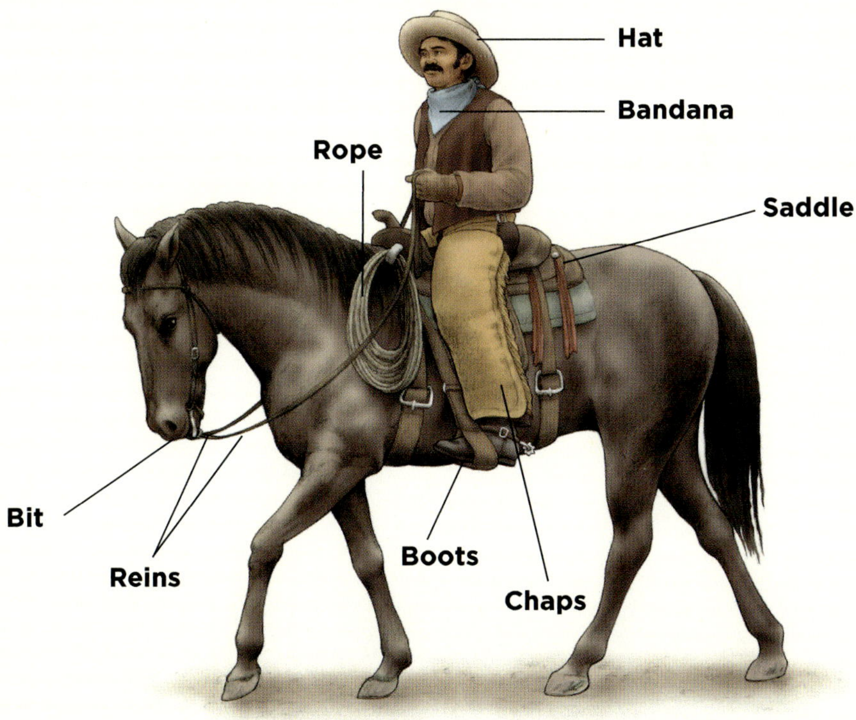

A COWBOY AND HIS EQUIPMENT

Cowboys wore special clothing to protect themselves from the weather. They used special equipment to do their job.

In the 1800s and early 1900s, horses also worked in cities. They pulled wagons full of food from farms to cities. They also moved goods and people around. Horses pulled carts, wagons, and streetcars.

Horses created a lot of pollution. City streets were smelly and noisy.

Ingram Publishing

Pony Express riders rode in all weather.

Traveling in cities was slow and **inefficient**. There were traffic jams and accidents because there were so many horses and carts. However, safety got better when road rules were created in the early 1900s.

Another way that horses worked was by carrying messages. Horses have helped people send messages for thousands of years. In 1860, the United States started a mail service called the Pony Express. The Pony Express delivered letters to **remote**, or far-off, areas.

The Pony Express did not last long. A telegraph line across the continent replaced it in 1861.

STOP AND CHECK

What work did horses do in cities?

CHAPTER THREE

Horses Today

In some places, horses are not used for work as much as they used to be. But in other areas, they still do some of the same jobs.

Horses are still used for transportation and milk in Kazakhstan and Mongolia. They are also still used for transportation in parts of Europe.

Horses even work on modern ranches. They are very helpful when the **terrain** is rough. This is because horses are easy to use when herding cattle over uneven ground.

The horses that cowboys and cowgirls use must be very well trained.

H.FougPre/Iconotec/Age Fotostock

There are many new jobs that horses do. One is equine therapy. Physically challenged people can learn to ride horses. Riding can help to make the people stronger and more coordinated.

Miniature, or very small, horses can help guide visually impaired people. The people can easily reach these horses because they are so short.

Guide horses learn to lead their owners across busy streets and wherever they need to go. They spend some of their time indoors. They also have a yard and a shelter for when they are outside.

Guide horses are small enough to move around easily in public places.

William Thomas Cain/Getty Images News/Getty Images

These days, horses are mostly used for sports and fun. Some horse owners join clubs or sports groups.

Many clubs teach young people about horses. Young riders learn to care for and ride their horses. They learn about their horses' **behavior**, or how horses act and respond. Riders also compete in events such as jumping, **dressage**, and grooming.

In jumping events, horse and rider go carefully but quickly to earn points.

George Doyle/Stockbyte/Getty Images

As in the past, horse riders compete with each other. Today, there are plowing races for farm horses. There are also galloping races for **thoroughbreds**.

Another competition is a horse triathlon. The events are dressage, racing, and jumping. These skills were once used in battle.

Reining is another sport based on the past. A rider guides the horse in circles at different speeds. This competition needs careful **manipulation**, or controlled movements, of the reins. These skills were needed in cattle ranching.

Dressage is sometimes called "horse ballet."

Polo horses must be very fit.

Karl Weatherly/Photodisc/Getty Images

The game of polo is played in teams of four riders and their horses. It is a fast and exciting game. Players use long wooden sticks called mallets. They try to hit a small ball between goalposts. The horses must be able to stop, start, and turn quickly.

STOP AND CHECK

What are some activities for horses and riders?

Conclusion

There has been a close bond between humans and horses for thousands of years. Horses changed how people worked, traveled, traded, and went to war.

Horses are no longer only working animals. People enjoy them and use them for fun and relaxation.

Domesticating horses changed the lives of ancient people. We continue to find more uses for horses in modern times.

There can be a close bond between a horse and its owner.

Respond to Reading

Summarize

Use key details to summarize *How Horses Changed the World*. Your graphic organizer may help you.

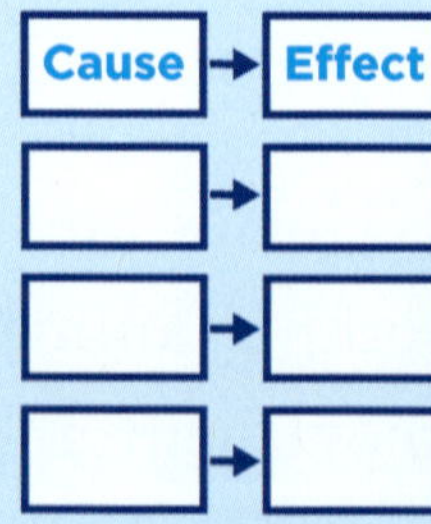

Text Evidence

1. What happened when people first domesticated horses as work animals? **CAUSE AND EFFECT**

2. Find the word *strays* on page 6. What clues help you to figure out the word's meaning? **VOCABULARY**

3. Reread Chapter 2. Write about two ways horses affected people's lives in the 1800s. **WRITE ABOUT READING**

Genre Expository Text

Compare Texts

Read about how an ancient food has benefits for us today.

From Cacao to Chocolate

Can you imagine a world without chocolate? There would be no chocolate chip cookies!

Cacao trees were discovered in South America thousands of years ago. A group of people called the Olmecs were the first to domesticate the trees. When they realized that the fruit was **edible**, they began to grow cacao trees as a crop.

The best part of the cacao fruit is in the center. This is where you find the cacao seeds.

The scientific name of cacao means "food of the gods."

The Olmecs made the first chocolate drinks. They pounded the cacao seeds. Then they added water and spices.

In 1519, an explorer named Hernando Cortés took cacao beans back to Europe. At some point, the word cacao became cocoa. This **mutated** form is the word we use today.

Many people believed that chocolate had healthful **nutrients**. In the 1700s, chocolate shops in London sold hot chocolate for high prices. Then machines were invented to grind the beans. Chocolate became cheaper.

(bkgd) Wetzel and Company, (b) John A. Rizzo/Photodisc/Getty Images

Today, chocolate is used in some of the world's most loved foods and drinks.

Chocolate is grown all over the world. Nearly 4 million tons of chocolate are produced each year. It is so popular that it is unlikely there will ever be a **surplus**.

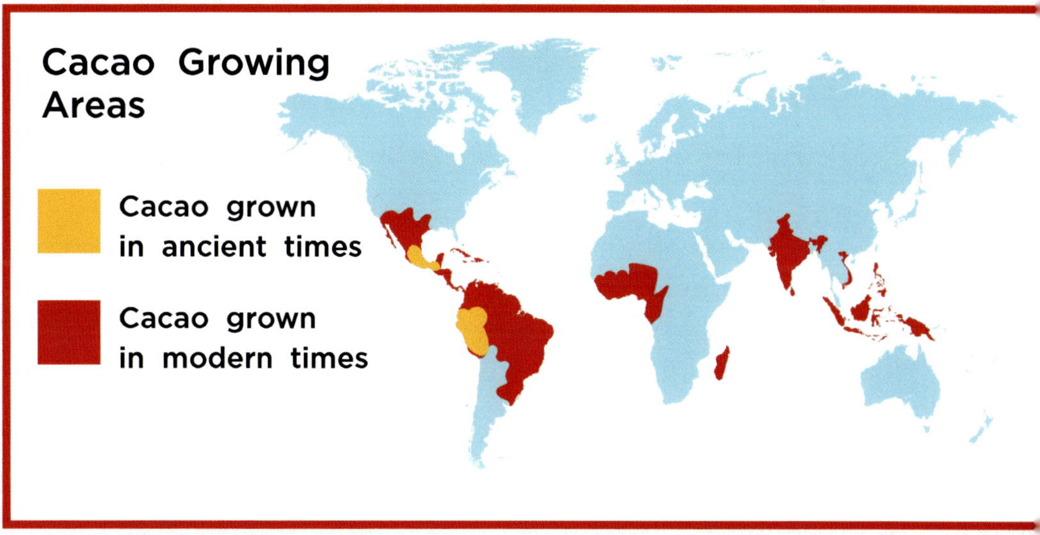

Make Connections

How did domesticating cacao lead to benefits for us today? **ESSENTIAL QUESTION**

In *How Horses Changed the World* and *From Cacao to Chocolate*, how do domesticated animals and plants benefit people? **TEXT TO TEXT**

Glossary

bit *(bit)* a piece of steel inserted into a horse's mouth and attached to the reins; a rider uses the reins and bit to guide and control the horse ***(page 3)***

bred *(bred)* raised animals to produce a new or better kind ***(page 3)***

domesticated *(duh-MES-ti-kayt-uhd)* changed from wild to tame in order to be useful for humans ***(page 2)***

dressage *(druh-SAHZH)* a competition in which horses perform special movements in response to signals from their riders ***(page 14)***

edible *(ED-uh-buhl)* fit to be eaten ***(page 19)***

spoked wheels *(spohkd hweelz)* wheels containing bars radiating from the center to the rim; lighter than a solid wheel ***(page 4)***

thoroughbreds *(THUR-uh-bredz)* animals bred from the best ancestors through many generations ***(page 15)***

Index

Focus on Social Studies

Purpose To explore how people have benefited from domesticating animals

What to Do

Step 1 Work in pairs or in groups. Talk about what you learned from *How Horses Changed the World*. Talk about the pros and cons of having horses as work animals.

Step 2 Choose another domesticated animal. Find out more about the animal. When did people first domesticate this animal?

Step 3 Discuss how domesticating your animal has helped people.